MY JOURNEY

By Ana C. Dávila

TRUE PERSPECTIVE
PUBLISHING HOUSE

AUTOGRAPH PAGE

Autograph this book to someone who is on a journey and
needs some encouragement along the way

TABLE OF CONTENTS

INTRODUCTION

My name is Ana Cecilia Perez Latorre and I was born in Santurce, Puerto Rico in 1967. I would like to share with you through this book what God has done in my life by means of an accident. Since then, I have had fifteen surgeries. In this book, I will share with you some of them specifically and the experience I have encountered. Before, I knew of the Lord, but in truth, I didn't personally know the Lord. It's totally two different things to know of God and to know God. Through this book I would like to narrate how God transformed the rebelliousness I felt toward Him, and how He changed my life and marriage.

Through this book your life will be ministered. How you can be firm in the midst of the desert you are going through, your loneliness and situations in your life. You will gain knowledge of how God maintains you strong and lifts you when you feel you are fading away. I learned to carry my life in the desert I have endured and how to maintain my obedience and strength before the Lord.

God had a calling in my life in spite of me not willing to accept it because of my rebelliousness. I had to pay the consequences for my disobedience. The reason I was inspired to write this book for you is because I wish for every person to learn that with God when things seem difficult, holding on to His hand everything is possible and you will reach victory. There's a verse I have made my own and I would like for you to make yours:

When you pass through the waters,
  I will be with you;
and when you pass through the rivers,
  they will not sweep over you.
When you walk through the fire,
  you will not be burned;
  the flames will not set you ablaze.
Isaiah 43:2 (NIV)

I began this book of "My Journey" on October 28th, 2011 in the middle of the recovery of my ankle implant. May the Lord bless you greatly and I pray this book is of great blessing to your life.

God bless,
Pastor Ana C. Dávila

DEDICATION

I would like to first and foremost to dedicate this work to my God who has given me the knowledge and understanding to bring my experiences to the Hispanic population and other languages. To my husband, Pastor Ramón Dávila for helping me one hundred percent in everything and for being with me in all stages of my surgeries, and for helping me publish this book. To my children Lilliana M. Dávila, Samuel A. Dávila and Alexandra E. Dávila because one way or the other, even though they didn´t understand what was going on, in their own understanding were always with me.

To Dr. Robert Hoover II for being with me for sixteen consecutive years. The Lord put him in my path to utilize his hands for the healing of my leg and to bring me support. To my mother in law Isabel Sánchez Pica for her support to push forward. To someone I love very much and who was with me from the beginning of this journey Belinda Garcia, thank you! I owe this to you for your support that you have given mc all these years.

To Alba López, María Collazo and Leticia López I don't know how to repay you for being by my side in good times and in difficult times. Thank you Pastor Martha Rolón for all the support you provided through all my surgeries. May the Lord continue to bless you! To all the members of our church "Iglesia Nueva Vida de Orlando", thank you for your nonstop prayers and support. To all my friends and Pastors who sustained me in prayer and who were with me every step of the way. I have no words to express my gratitude.

May the Lord continue to bless you.
I love you,

Pastor Ana C. Dávila

CHAPTER ONE:

<u>My Rebelliousness</u>

Allow me to start by telling you that many times when we go through difficulties in our lives we always blame God for things that occur to us. I am not here to give accounts of my biography, I am here to share my testimony. How God transformed me when I had lost all hope in my life and didn't want anything to do with God.

In my adolescence, things happened which I did not understand. One of these was when my stepfather had sexually abused me when I was about 11 years old. It was very heart breaking when trying to speak to my mother about what had happened to me and she didn't express the minimum interest. She didn't lend me her attention and in many other times she simply didn't want to hear me out. At age 13 my grandmother passes, she was who cared for me since my infancy. Her death pained me deeply, I was very close to her.

At age 18 my mother dies, this was much unexpected. In the midst of everything I was attending church and had been baptized when I was 12 years old. I was the instrument the Lord utilized to bring my mother to His path. At the same time, I was angry with the Lord. I didn't understand why I had to go through all of this and I didn't want to have anything to do with God, church or religion. I didn't understand why my mother had me responsible over my brother when I was only 9 years old. Why I had to be sexually abused and had my childhood and youthfulness robbed. I didn't understand why my mother had to die when I was just 18. I found myself alone, abandoned. I needed her in my life, as I was recently married.

> **Psalm 27:10** (NIV)
> *"Though my father and mother forsake me,*
> *the Lord will receive me."*

It doesn't matter how many people you have surrounding you, many times you will feel alone. The Lord is so great and marvelous He did not permit that I remain alone. At age 14, I met a handsome and beautiful boyfriend. God had a plan for my life. Before my mother had passed away the Lord had allowed me to marry him at age 18. At the same time in my heart there was a seed which I did not allow to germinate. Many times we hear about God and the seed sown into our hearts, but we don't allow it to germinate in our lives.

In all my rebelliousness, The Lord blessed me with a husband that respected me in spite of knowing about my sexual abuse. We married when I was 18 years of age on December 24, 1985. On February 20, 1986 my mom dies. I mention all this because through it all God had a plan already established for my life. I wasn't left alone with no course, He gave me a partner, since I had no other family members.

Do you know why I want to share with you part of my history? Because it doesn't matter what you have been through or the difficulties you have endured, God has a perfect plan even though you don't understand it and don't perceive it now. I was in rebelliousness for many years, all while worshipping and assisting church. But now is when it gets better, because in the next chapter we will continue with the rebellion, but in a different way. Many times people may demonstrate that they are Christians before others, but before the Lord in their hearts, they're really not.

I did not use drugs, abuse alcohol or any other vice, but I had a void my heart I wanted to fill especially with material things. In my rebelliousness I attempted suicide with pills at the age of 14. Because when you are most destroyed, depressed, and in your mind you say to yourself that you are useless, is when the enemy puts negative thoughts in your mind to tear you apart and lead you to death. The Lord in His infinite mercy rescued and delivered me from death. He had already chosen me from my mother's womb.

Psalm 18:30
"As for God, his way is perfect: The Lord's word is flawless: He shields all who take refuge in him."

This bible verse wants to communicate no matter how rebellious or how far you want to run from the Lord, His ways are perfect and He will always keep you.

CHAPTER 2:

R<small>EBELLIOUS</small> B<small>EFORE THE</small> P<small>LANS</small>

I met my husband at age 14, and our relationship was not easy. But because it was part of the Lord's purpose, the enemy wanted to chime in. As I mentioned before, we married in December 24, 1985 against my mother's wishes, but The Lord had a plan for my life. Do you know why? Because everything God allows to happen in our lives is part of His perfect plan. When my mother dies in 1986, I met my biological father. Previous to this I never knew of him. This caused a deep impression in my life, this was part of the emptiness in my heart.

After a period of many events, I married and went directly to Patuxent River, Maryland because my husband had found work there. Imagine me at age 18, not knowing a word of English, not knowing how to drive, stuck in the fields, I was so young. Imagine a country girl from Guayama Puerto Rico in foreign territory that I was not accustomed to. This is how The Lord works when He has a plan for you. Regardless of where you are going or how you feel He will accomplish it no matter what.

I lived in Maryland for one and half years. Thank be to God, after that one and half years my husband found work in Florida, sometimes called "Fantasy Land". Before we moved, I was fighting with The Lord all the time. In spite of not wanting to have anything to do with Him, I did want to leave the state. Again I say, God had a perfect plan in our lives. And that God that I didn't want in my life, answered my prayers when that same day my husband receives a call from Florida and accepts a job without knowing what type of work it was. The funny part is that he calls me on the telephone and he informs me and I begin to scream and at the same time to cry and I went to the foot of my bed to give thanks to God for answering me.

When my husband got home from work I had all our belongings collected and many things of the apartment in boxes. If it wasn't for the hand of God, my marriage would have ended in divorce. That's exactly what the enemy had planned for my marriage. In that very instance I asked God for forgiveness. When you come with a contrite and humble heart before the Lord, He will recognize you in public.

CHAPTER 3:

MOVING TO FLORIDA AND THE CALLING

Now is when our journey begins and look at what God was doing. We moved to Central Florida in June 1987. We arrived in Florida and we started working, my husband in the Naval Training Center and me at Burger King as a cashier not knowing a word of English. We started visiting a Presbyterian church where we became members.

Yet my heart was empty, I didn't feel what I heard other people say they were feeling in the presence of the Lord and the anointing of the Lord in my life. The reason I mention this is because where I had been baptized the Lord had already sewn a seed in my heart. It was at the Baptist Church of Carolina, Puerto Rico. There was a separate bible study group where I felt the presence of The Lord and a beautiful anointing. I knew what it was to feel Him. I knew about angelical tongues, I knew what malice was. Even though I knew all these things I was still rebellious because I knew of Him, but did not know Him.

At this Presbyterian church, the three children The Lord pleased to give us were born; Lilliana, Samuel and Alexandra. In this church we persevered nine straight years without knowing the Lord was equipping me little by little. I started singing with the church choir and teaching bible school to the children. My husband started teaching bible school to the adults. At the same time, he was an "Elder" and he also preached every now and then. It was a technique of God Almighty equipping us for what He had prepared.

After nine years in the Presbyterian Church, The Lord personally calls on my husband to start a work, a ministry. I didn't want to accept it because I knew the commitment and sacrifice that was required before the Lord. Well, with many difficulties and problems that the enemy had put before our path, God at the same time was opening doors. Let me tell you when God calls on you, no man, neither council, nor anyone that can stop what God wants to do with you.

The Lord opened doors for us to acquire a location for our ministry on Lake Underhill Road in Orlando; all good and nice although there some opposition and some people that were not satisfied, but most important was my husband's humbleness and the support of our God. The Lord permitted the doors to our ministry to open Sunday, January 4th, 1998. I didn't feel part of the ministry and consequently I simply didn't want to be there. My children played sports in and out of school. So every time they had a game I would go with them so I wouldn't have to go to church with my husband, much less help him or play the part of the pastor's wife. I knew my husband suffered but I was so blind that I didn't realize what I was doing. In many occasions, I threatened to burn his office to ashes because I detested Christian music and Christian books. I didn't feel in my heart to serve the Lord with a life as hectic as mine.

Do you know what it feels like to be exposed at everyone's critique because you're not playing the role of a pastor or pastor's wife? What I'm trying to say is nine years in the Presbyterian Church and now starting a ministry was not easy. God had to perform his work and he needed to squeeze me, because I didn't understand. Yet above all I feared the Lord and I knew there was a great God. We served for nine years at this church on Lake Underhill Road where God was still equipping us for the revolution that He was going to do with us.

CHAPTER 4:

THE BLESSING OF PROSPERING

In the year 2000, she who did not know the English language, a country girl from Guayama, Puerto Rico started working as a teacher's assistant in an elementary school. Imagine how big this was for me! I could not believe I had passed an interview in English. WOW! I recognized that the Lord was great. Let me tell you, never in my life I thought I would have a job in an elementary school. This was way above me. Because when I was a child, for my mother nothing I did was right and I had many insecurities in my life that the Lord needed to heal so I could reach the goal and spiritual level He wanted me in. Do not allow other people to stop what you want to do in your life. The only thing that matters is that you are in agreement with God, not your family or friends.

I started working that year as a kindergarten teacher's assistant. It was very difficult to work with another language and a culture different from your own, but God was in control. Through all of this I was still rebellious against the Lord. Make no mistake! At work, I met a servant of God, Belinda Garcia. From the moment I met her she was always confessing to me that I was a Pastor. She urged me not to run away from God's calling in my life. Every time I saw her at work I tried to dodge her so she would leave me alone. I didn't feel like talking to anyone about the Lord. At that time when I met Belinda, she was Pentecostal with some doctrines of men. Through her the Lord started ministering to my life in different areas and as the years went by we became the best of friends. The Lord had utilized her as an instrument in my life in such a big way and we're still great friends. So much so, she was the youth pastor at our Church. I am always grateful to God for the small grain that "Belly" put in my life.

At work, I started to prosper as a person and I progressed in learning the English language. In August of 2001, there was an opening in the school office for a bilingual person. I would never had applied for the position because inside me I knew I wasn't prepared for the position. But because God knows all things look what happened, without me noticing the school secretary puts a notice in my mailbox to advise me at what time the interview for the opening will take place. I go to her and say: *"I'm no good for this"*, but she says that I'm the perfect candidate. So, I went to the interview shaking from the nerves.

Let me tell you, in many occasions we pray only when we are in need, before taking a test, job interviews or in any situation in your life. We proclaim we are Christians, but it's to our convenience. A week and one half had passed after I was interviewed, waiting on the decision of who was going to fill the position. In case you didn't know, I wasn't the only one that was interviewed. There were other candidates more qualified than me both in the English language and in computer skills. But the Lord had His plans and was in control. I was chosen for the office position, yet in my rebellion I was grateful to the Lord because I never thought I would work in an office and much less at the front desk where I am the first face you see when walking in. WOW! God is good all the time and all the time God is good! Never doubt what the Lord is going to do with you even when things are not in your favor.

CHAPTER 5:

THE ACCIDENT (THE BLOW)

I started working in the office and as a kindergarten teacher's assistant until they found my replacement. In the mornings as an assistant and in the afternoon in the office as part of the training. On October 18th, 2001 I was painting the porch ceiling of my home and I am terrified of wasps. There were three wasps that were hovering around me. I had already stepped off the aluminum ladder twice to get the poison and kill them. On the third try, I didn't realize I had skipped two steps to get down. As the saying goes, "Third time's the charm!". When I came down the last time, I came down with such force that my left ankle was in a lot of pain. Inadvertently, my left ankle was caught behind the ladder and trying to set it free I fell to the side. Thank God I put my hand on my temple because when I fell to the side I hit my head against the front steps of our house. If it wasn't for that I wouldn't be recounting this. I started screaming of the unbearable pain. When I fell I snapped my ankle, it was dangling and swollen. My husband was painting the back of the house when he heard my screams. He didn't realize what had happened, he thought I was yelling about the wasps and he delayed to get to the front of the house. While I was laying on the floor, my oldest daughter called a friend of ours who lives five minutes away from our house. I remember she got to our house in a robe and curlers. She sat me on a chair and tried to take off my sneaker. My husband after putting everything away, came to try to lift me and take me to the car because in our house we had no crutches or a wheel chair. It's funny because from that moment on God started to deal with me. When we made it to the hospital my husband brought me a wheel chair, while I was crying because of the intense pain I was feeling. First, the nurse said: *"I need a urine sample"*, I said to my husband: *"How? I can't go to the bathroom in this pain!"* My husband had to go with me to the women's bathroom and help me with everything. This was hilarious because while my husband was in the bathroom, two other women entered. First I was taken to a examination room, and after I was taken to get x-rays of my ankle, which was still dangling. Then I was taken back to the examination room and I was given an I.V. with a pain sedative. All of the sudden, I heard many people talking around me. The doctor who was attending that afternoon in the emergency room gets close to my face and says: *"Mrs., were going to try to reposition your ankle back in place. But if we do and there isn't any circulation to your foot and ankle you're going to have surgery immediately. If we reposition and there's circulation, we'll immobilize it and have you see a specialist".* In my mind with all the pain, I was pleading to God for them not to operate me that night. Here's the process; a nurse held my thigh very tight, another nurse held my knee and leg and the doctor repositioned the ankle in place. Brothers and sisters I was going through such a horrible pain and I felt when it snapped in place. It's like when your car needs fixing and a part is being replaced. I was in such pain I saw angels and stars of all sorts of colors, HAHAHA!! Thank God I didn't need surgery that night and my foot was immobilized from the knee down to my ankle and foot because I had circulation. I still didn't understand why this had happened to me. I kept saying to the Lord *"I don't cause harm to anyone, I help people, I don't deserve this."* I questioned God: *"Why me? Why not other people that do deserve this?"* Many times people do not wish to hear that God is talking to them because they feel they're good and don't cause harm to anyone. Like I was saying, the reason why I couldn't have surgery (besides the blood circulation) was because my foot was very swollen. It felt like a volcano when it heats up and it's ready to erupt from any place. So, on my foot and ankle I had water blisters as if I had been burned. Specifically, I had a big blister on the right side of my ankle which I couldn't burst because I could have gotten a really bad infection. The pain from that blister was driving me crazy and didn't allow me to sleep!

Meanwhile, my husband searched for a foot and ankle specialist which we visited. The office was called "Foot and Ankle Associates". The first doctor we saw said: *"That's a tremendous trauma for the ankle and it wasn't going to heal well"* and he couldn't do the surgery by himself. He wanted another doctor to assist, but he was away. So we got an appointment for the following week. I was still in horrible pain, I had a cast that kept my ankle immobilized. Before I continue, never accept a negative word from someone and much less when it comes it's related to your health.

> Psalms 37:5 says: *"Commit thy way unto the Lord; trust also in him; and he shall bring it to pass"*.

OK, back to my story; when the other specialist Dr. Robert Hoover II saw me he said: *"Do you know the trauma that you have on that ankle? I'm going to have to reconstruct it. Let's wait a little because it's still very swollen"*. The reason was that if he operated now he wouldn't be able to stitch it because of the swollenness. Like a very stubborn and disobedient person, I didn't want to understand I couldn't be useful in my situation.

I got up on my crutches to season a chicken and cook when I should have been resting waiting for my swelling to go down. And like every disobedient person, I paid the consequences. While seasoning the chicken I started arguing with my children because they didn't realize what I was going through. I fell to the floor with crutches and all. The next day my husband had to take me back to the doctor.

The date of the surgery was pushed up because I managed to completely destroy my ankle more than it was before because of my stubbornness. Let me say, that's how the Lord is toward us. He deals with you, wants to enter your heart and transforms you. Many times we don't allow God to work because of our egos and our stubbornness. This is why many times we must pay the consequences of our disobedience.

> *The Lord your God is with you,*
> *the Mighty Warrior who saves.*
> *He will take great delight in you;*
> *in his love he will no longer rebuke you*
> *but will rejoice over you with singing."*
> **Zephaniah 3:17 (KJV)**

CHAPTER 6:

Reconstruction of My Ankle and My Life

So it is on October 18th, 2001 when I had my accident and I had my ankle surgery on October 31st, 2001. The day of my surgery came and I was clearly very nervous and in much pain. My husband, my doctor and myself together we prayed for the surgery. My doctor is a Christian. The surgery lasted for a full six hours. When the doctor cut open, he discovered it was worse than the x-rays had shown. The bones of my ankle had shredded to pieces; some to the size of rice grains. He had to utilize a tourniquet because he had to put it back piece by piece. Also, he had to insert a piece of bone from a cadaver since there was too much of a gap and it needed to be filled.

When the surgery was done the doctor sent me to the hospital for a night due to the surgery lasting so long. Normally, he operates in an outpatient clinic. He sent me to the hospital in an ambulance until the next day. OH LORD! Such pain! Even with the morphine the pain was immense! At this point in my life this surgery was the biggest thing that had ever happen to me.

My husband cried while saying: *"I feel like I'm living a nightmare!"* All I did was cry desperately in pain and ask myself *"why has this happened to me?"*, without understanding.

The wound was so big that I had ten stitches on each side of the ankle and I still had the water blisters. I felt it throbbing and pulsing. I bit into pillows, stuffed animals, anything that helped alleviate the pain and the throbbing. I arrived home from the hospital and that's when the Lord started to transform my life and began my recuperation.

My children and me, this picture was taken in Washington, DC while in recovery.

CHAPTER 7:

RECOVERY AND DIVINE VISITATION

In my first visit with the doctor after the surgery, my bandages were removed to see my wound and have my bandages replaced. Brothers and sisters you can't imagine the pain that I was in, because no one could touch it. I couldn't stop crying! When we got to the house from the hospital the next evening, my husband was throwing himself on me crying and saying *"I'm living a nightmare!"*. I was questioning God with tears in my eyes "Why me Lord?", "I don't believe I deserve this!"

In the interim while I was home recuperating, the Lord came to visit me one night. I was about to take my life. In my ignorance I didn't understand the why so much pain. Even though I knew of God, I took many pain pills to see if something would happen because I wanted to die. I didn't want to go through this pain. I wasn't a bad daughter, a bad wife or a bad mother. That night I felt in my body the presence of the Lord touching my heart and hearing His voice which said: "I am with you".

When they took off the bandage on my second visit, almost two weeks after the surgery it was replaced with a cast. I remember my ankle being purple in color and how much it hurt! When they put on the cast I still had the water blister I had mentioned, it had not yet burst. When they put on the cast, the blister and my foot caused my whole foot to throb and be in much pain. I was in bed for four months. Alone in my room as time went by, I cried and spoke to the Lord. I asked for forgiveness for my disobedience. That's when I truly understood what had happened to me was because of my disobedience. I understood that my life had a purpose for Him. There I started pleading for forgiveness because I was fleeing from the calling he had for my life. There He started cleansing my heart of resentment, bitterness and rebelliousness from my past. I asked my husband for forgiveness for threatening to burn his office. And there in those months, the Lord started my transformation. Don't wait for the Lord to give you a blow for you to be obedient to the calling He has placed for your life.

The Lord started transforming my life through praise and worship. In that moment in my life He needed to work not only in the spiritual, but also in the daily living. In my character and the resentment that I carried in my heart, the bitterness, sadness and I had to accept Ana, the real Ana. I never had a personal encounter with the Lord in church, many times it was emotional and with this you must be cautious. I had a personal encounter with the Lord in my room through Christian music, praise and worship. Many times the experience that people have with the Lord when they go to a conference, a retreat or church, and they come to the front is emotional. Because they are going through a situation or a necessity at that moment and the majority of the times is emotional.

At this time the Lord started teaching me how to depend on people like my husband. How difficult it is when you feel auto sufficient (Wonder Woman) and have to depend on other people. Do you know why? I had to learn how to depend on God, and God through others took care of me. You will also find those who instead of helping, they hinder you. For example; I had a visit from a couple and the lady tells me: *"Oh, something similar happened to my cousin and they had to cut her leg off"*.

Brothers and sisters don't let the enemy sift you and put negative thoughts in your head. Because what the enemy wants is to make you sad when you are going through a situation and lead you to depression. Through all of this they held my position at my job. I started working again on February 4, 2002 in crutches and not able to firmly stand or walk on my foot.

At that time, I went to 52 therapies, when I started walking again it was like when a baby begins to walk. Very much like when you meet the Lord and give yourself to Him completely. You start to walk like a baby because you're learning while you walk in the word of God. Honestly, let me say all of this was not easy. But by holding on to the hand of God I made it to victory. The reconstruction was not the end of it, my ankle was in pain all the time and I learned to live in pain.

Psalms 73:26 (KJV)
"My flesh and my heart may fail,
but God is the strength of my heart
and my portion forever".

September 15th, 2006 I had another surgery to relocate my bones into place. I had a metal rod on the right side of my left leg. It wasn't a rod on the inside, it was a long rod on the outside with pins on the side of the leg. Brothers and sisters in my wheel chair, with that metal rod sticking out of my leg I cooked meals. WOW! I sometimes look back and don't know how I did it! Two months after the surgery I returned to work in a wheel chair with that rod sticking out and my leg lifted. If I made the effort to go to work like that, it was because I had a commitment with my job. How would I not be able to do it for the Lord! When He was the one who gave me strength and endurance to continue forward. I had that metal rod attached to my leg for three full months.

That rod caused me so much pain. At the same time, I felt like I had a sting in the spiritual realm without knowing when it will end.

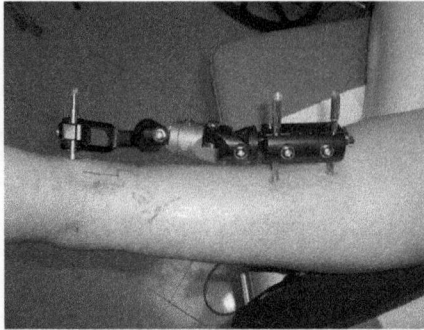

My left leg with the "external fixator"

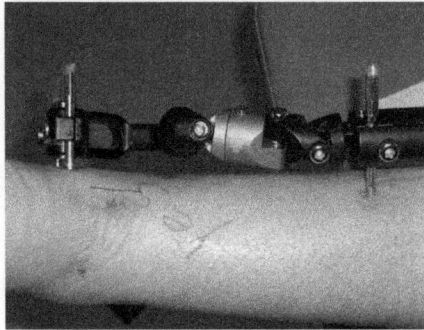

My left leg with the "external fixator". This is how I went to work.

CHAPTER 8:

THE PROCESS

Well, that Ana that didn't want to be at church or help her husband had to go through a mishap with her ankle in order for God to start His process in her. After the accident and during the process of recuperation the Lord started to utilize me as an instrument while being in my wheel chair, to minister other people through the Holy Spirit and sometimes I couldn't believe it myself.

Soon after, the Lord started revealing beautiful things and giving me discernment to the glory of the Lord. But before this happened in my life, in my own church I felt lost. In my heart and in my soul I desired more. The Lord permitted that Belinda Garcia pesters me at work. Belinda was a servant of God that called me Pastor and pester me, because when I met her I didn't want to have anything to do with the Lord or my obligations. Many times the Lord used her and continues to use her because she is a tremendous woman of God.

The Lord put in my path Pastor Marie Sandoz to speak and lift me spiritually confirming the calling God had for my life. I had yet to accept the calling of pastor in my life because of the fear inside me. And the church which my husband pastored wasn't going to accept it either. Through all of this, the Lord was also ministering to my husband removing some religious traditions that were still in him. Well, the Lord is so good and powerful that after this surgery, and some other surgeries, Pastor Marie Sandoz was the first person to speak to me about preaching in a conference about abuse in a "Women's Conference". The ministry was called "Transformed Women". WOW! This for me was huge! Me standing in an altar to preach to a bunch of women about abuse. Notice how the Lord was already working with me since childhood, I had to go through sexual abuse and in the process of adulthood, the Lord would heal me in order for me to speak about different types of abuse.

Let me tell you, many times you say you forgive or I forgive them but when you remember these situations you begin to cry with sentiment and anger. This means you have not healed inside. This for me was a challenge brothers and sisters, because I wished and desired for my step father to die or become very ill so he would suffer. But the Lord had already healed me so I would be able to speak about this situation. In that conference, the Lord opened my husband's eyes about the calling He had over my life. But it didn't end there! I cried tears of blood for how God had to utilize me. My husband did not want to accept it.

We shared the facility with the Presbyterian church for nine years until the Lord said: *"I will move you from here"*. My husband did not believe me. He thought I was crazy and I didn't know what I was saying. It's difficult to believe someone, much less if it's your wife, who insulted you, threatened you and was always bitter. It was difficult for him to accept that the Lord had given her a pastoral calling, and more so that the Lord had transformed her. But that's what it was, already the American church was persecuting and prohibiting many things in their facility. But God permitted it, and it's purpose was for my husband to trust and depend in the Lord even more. Whenever the Lord asks you to do something for Him, you will always have persecution and will always have obstacles.

CHAPTER 9:

THE MOVING AND THE ACCEPTANCE OF MY CALLING

The moment arrived to move to another facility in 2008. Before the beginning of the New Year we were in our new location. The Lord moved us and started a church completely independent. In our new location on Hanging Moss Road in Orlando, God started to do great things. We started opening a prayer service on Tuesday and the youth ministry started to grow. There the Lord started to minister to my husband about the calling He had set for over my life. He began to accept it and put up signs of Pastor Ramón and Ana C. Dávila.

In the beginning, it was a hard process for me to know that my husband didn't recognize the pastoral calling that God had put in me since very young. This is why you ask yourself: *"why did these processes have to happen in my life?"* And it's because God had already chosen you from your mother's womb to serve Him so you can give an account of these processes to others through the word of God and reveal to others where God had taken you from. The Lord revealed to my husband my pastoral calling and he started accepting the transformation that God had done in my life.

As pastors, the Lord was taking us to a new and beautiful spiritual dimension and as a couple. WOW! I could now worship without a time limit and without having to look at a clock, because previously my husband preached with a clock and our praise and worship chants were time set. God had to eliminate those things and He started with me. The tremendous anointing of the Holy Spirit was felt. Finally, when my calling is accepted new oppositions began which is a good thing, because through process is how we learn how to grow spiritually.

CHAPTER 10:

SECOND MOVE AND MY NEXT SURGERY

WOW! The Lord has a perfect plan for everything. He already gave me prior notice about this move. Brothers and sisters let me inform you that this will be surgery number eight after my accident. Through all these years from when I first got injured, the Lord kept polishing me more and more through my ankle surgeries. I understood that every time I had a surgery he would rest me because there were things He still had to work in me. Don't forget He starts from the inside out.

Remember that Satan is not going to be happy with what you do for God, and I had already surrendered my life to Him. While still at this church, having not moved yet, the Lord provided everything at all times for this small church. In Hanging Moss Road, God polished me in many areas of my life. Yet the pastor didn't want to be obedient to the Lord. He still wanted to be a lay pastor in the Presbyterian church. He didn't understand that was not what God wanted for him and His church.

The Lord wanted something else, another dimension for our church and that's what I was searching for; a church where I would receive and be filled with the Holy Spirit, the word of God in my life and heart. No doubt that the acceptance of my calling caused a revolution. Because when you have people surrounding you who do not believe in your calling, what they want is to see your head roll. They will talk about you whenever and wherever. But when you go to the presence of God, who called on you personally, there is no one or nothing that can take it away. Because who called you was God, and God will back you up.

In this location where we were, I had to go through another surgery to see if my bones could be repaired, because one of my bones was in bad shape. As I previously mentioned, for surgery number eight I had a metal rods piercing from side to side of my leg, from under my knee to the sole of my foot. WOW! That surgery for me was terrible. Five hours in the operating room and another week at the hospital just to soothe the pain. I drank my tears in pain, but at the hospital in the middle of my pain and suffering I sang the praise song that goes: "In the midst of my pain, In the midst of my suffering, there's a voice that says do not fear, I am with you". That praise song gave me strength and I felt the hand of God over me.

I knew this surgery had a purpose in God. I didn't understand why if I already was working for Him and had given my life to Him, I had to go through this process again. What the Lord had conveyed to my heart in midst of this pain was the pain He had to go through on the cross.;

when He was crucified without anesthesia, in the living flesh. I would give thanks to God because I knew and I felt just a little of what He suffered for you and for me. A round "external fixator" was placed around my leg. It was a hard process and I remember the pain was so immense sometimes I wanted to chop my leg off. I endured three months with those rods in my leg and with those rods I had to walk with a walker three times a day.

Every time I walked I said to the Lord: *"every step I take is a step of victory"*. I thank God for a sister in Christ who was with me many times during these weeks cooking and taking care of me. She was who helped me to walk and always encouraged me. God will never leave you in your moment of difficulty.

Every time I went to the doctor he had to adjust the rods in my bones to see if they were correctly fixed in position. He had to hit the rods with an instrument, kind of like a wrench, to make sure they were adjusted. Oh! How much it would hurt every time he tapped those rods, I felt everything. My doctor at that time was going through colon cancer.

Many times we wrote emails to each other to comfort each other in the Lord. I was away from my secular job for three months and the rods were removed on January 14th, 2010.

Allow me to say that in every moment God was in control. Although many times because we believe we are strong we think we are in control. I suffered through physical pain, but meanwhile the Lord was ministering to my life in a supernatural manner. God cleansed my heart and was molding my character to His resemblance. Sometimes we give God excuses for any reason, yet I am a person who loves to worship God. So with the rods, crutches, and in pain, I stood up front with the church worship group to praise my God. Do not, under any circumstance, stop worshipping and praising God above all things because He will give you the victory.

"Every step I take is a step of victory". Each time I said that out loud, declaring my healing, the Lord gave me new strength. In the next pages, you will see pictures showing the bandages that were needed for each perforation on my leg. The black mark on my heel and on my big toe was due to an allergic reaction to the anticoagulant medicine. This injection is injected in my stomach for a period of ten days. The black mark became an ulcer. That ulcer had to be opened and drained and It took more than a month to heal.

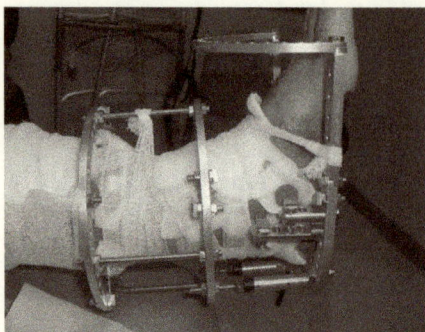

My leg with all the bandages 2 days after leaving the hospital.

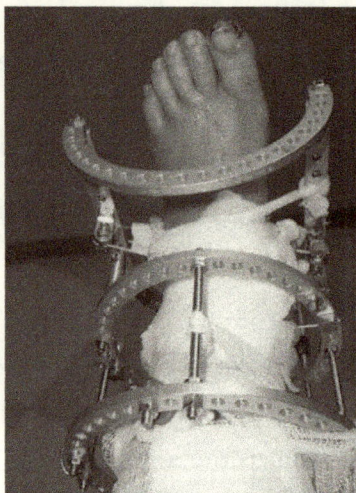

My leg with the bandages and the black spot on my big toe.

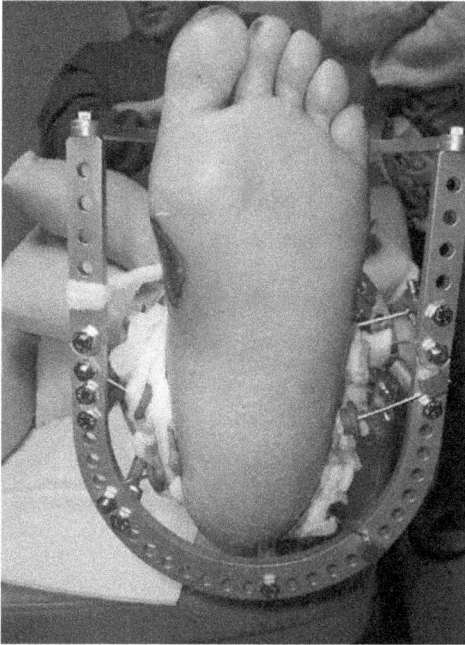

My foot with the bandages and the black spot on the sole of my foot that became an ulcer.

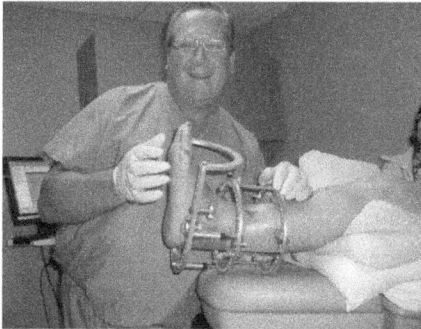

Dr. Hoover II who has been such a blessing for my life. I have been with him for the past fifteen years.

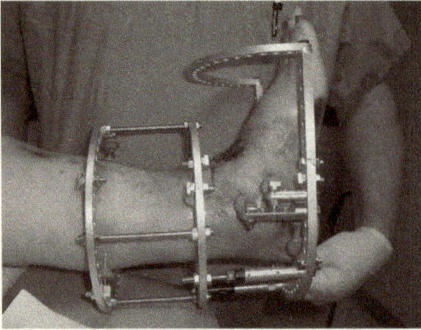

My leg without any bandages, this is when he tapped the pins that were piercing my leg. With a wrench used to fix cars, only smaller, he adjusted the pins and then cleaned them so they wouldn't stick to my skin. This was immense pain! I clenched to any part of my clothes or my husband's hand.

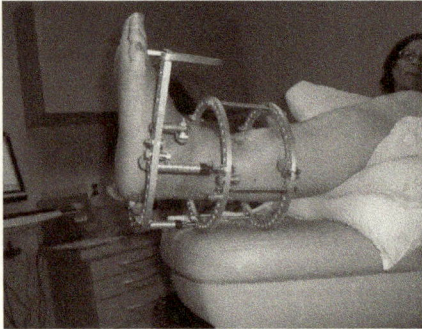

My left leg. With my friend who I would grip her hand while going through the pain.

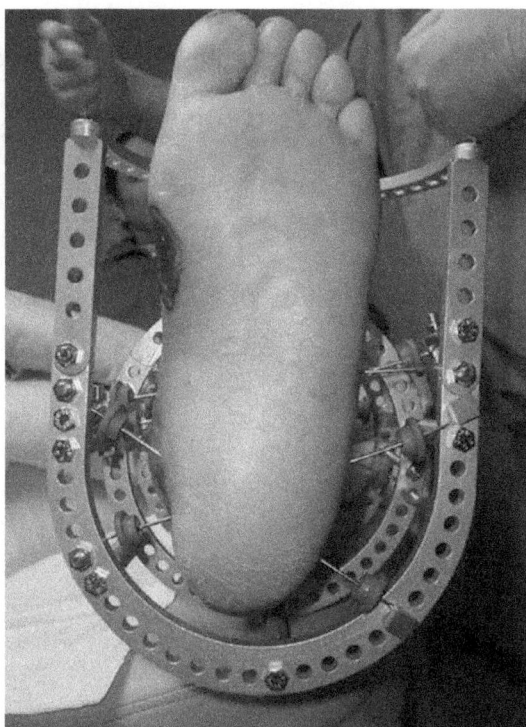

My foot without bandages showing the ulcer.

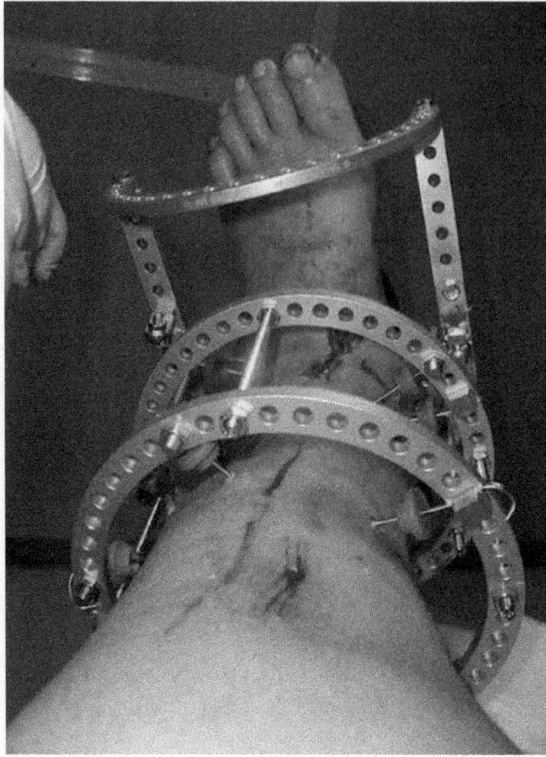

My leg completely without bandages.

This surgery was not easy, but it was harder when I had to start using a walker. The pain of putting my leg down and feeling the circulation felt like electric shocks throughout my whole leg. I have the scars but I remembered the Lord because He had scars, so for me to have them is nothing.

On December 29th, 2009, in the interim of three months we moved for the second time to a warehouse in Forsyth Road, Winter Park, FL. A warehouse that with God's provisions we were able to convert into a church. We are there now, still declaring the building which God promised us and will come.

CHAPTER 11:

THE CLEANSING

When we moved to this place which would make it our second move, the Lord was moving like never before. All of the sudden, The Lord had to clear out people who were not in agreement with the vision the Lord had given to us pastors and the church. Through the cleanup the Lord made, He had mercy on us. The pastors, leaders and the church went through many difficulties, sadness and broken hearts, but in the midst of the test, God was involved. I'm going to let you know when you have a rotten apple, let it be in the church, at work, or many times where you live, it's going to spoil the others when the vision is not followed. Let it be the pastors or the church, God has to remove them from the church so it can produce, prosper and continue moving forward with the promises God has given.

I'm not going to deny that in many cases I felt like I was going to fade away. I wanted to give up, take off my gloves and forget my calling and the ministry. But when going through those challenges the Lord gave me a word about the palm tree. It doesn't matter how many hurricanes force winds, tornadoes or thunderstorms try to shake the palm tree, it remains firm because its roots are deep. The roots may move, but not be rooted. What this means is it doesn't matter what others say about you and the difficulties you may endure, even if you have been shook, no one or nothing will remove you from your place.

What I want to say is just as the Lord performs a cleansing in a church, he also performs a cleansing in your heart and your character. Cleansings are necessary in order for a church to grow spiritually, and for people to grow spiritually. When people leave the church the majority use the excuse that they are not growing spiritually, but let me say that it is not the church which makes your grow, and I say it with experience.

What makes you grow is your intimate relationship with the Lord. If you do not have an intimate relationship with the Lord you're not going anywhere. In the middle of the cleansing, God had mercy. What I mean is He removed, but He also provided with new leaders and people who took charge of one of our ministries. Ministries that people left abandoned, but God was in control. If one day you leave your church for whatever reason, please let your pastors know. Don't leave without speaking to them or at least thanking them for what has been done for you. At that time, the Lord raised a sister which we care for deeply, Alba López. The Lord raised her to direct the dance and mime ministry in our church. I thank God for the cleansing, for He has allowed us to see His glory and showed us where we are headed.

"Remain firm like the palm tree"

CHAPTER 12:

MY NEXT SURGERY: ANKLE IMPLANT

On September 20th, 2011, I had my next surgery, it was my ankle implant. Nevertheless, the year 2011 was a difficult year for me. We started in May of 2011 with a small surgery to remove a cyst that emerged on the right side of my ankle. I had to go to Puerto Rico with much difficulty to preach at a women's conference. People, I didn't know how I got to Puerto Rico, but it was God who took me.

On August of 2011, I was hospitalized a week because I had a kidney stone. The reason for my hospitalization was because my kidneys were very swollen. I knew this wasn't God, we were about a week away from our church women's conference, but in that hospital bed I praised and worshipped God and declared myself healed. When I overcame that process within two weeks I had my ankle implant surgery that lasted five hours.

I was in the hospital for three days to recover. When I visited my doctor for the first time after this last surgery, the stitches were left in place for another three weeks. When they were removed I caught an infection. Because I am diabetic I had an open wound and you could see the tendons inside where the ankle bends. I was in recovery for three months without being able to walk. But praise God I got up and went to my secular job in a wheel chair two months after my recovery.

One thing I would like to share with you; if you hold a secular job and head to work in pain or with a serious wound don't go. If something were to happen, no one will appreciate the years you went to work in that condition. Do not over sacrifice in your secular job because at the end of the day if something happens to you, you'll be replaced the next day. Here are a few more photos of my ankle implant which I currently have.

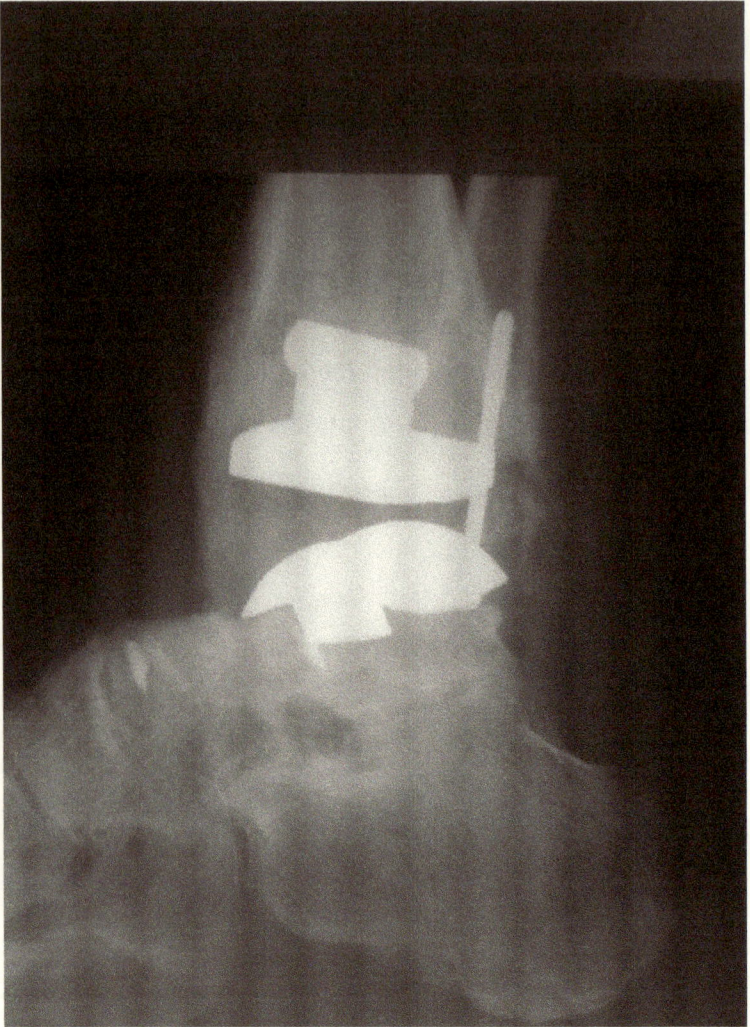

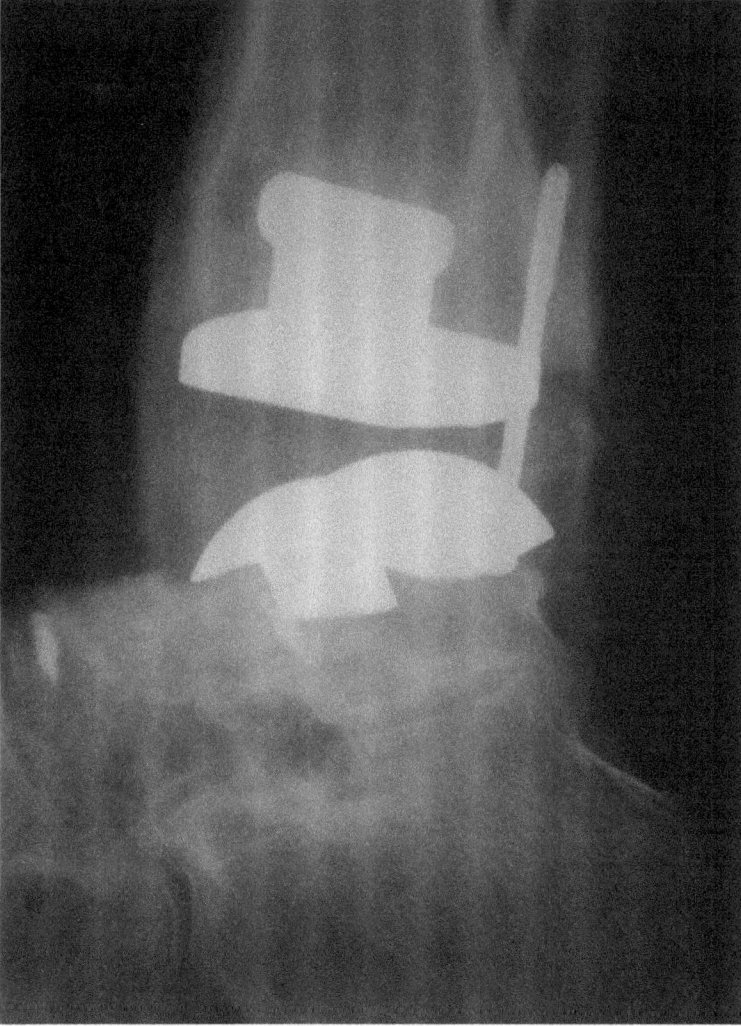

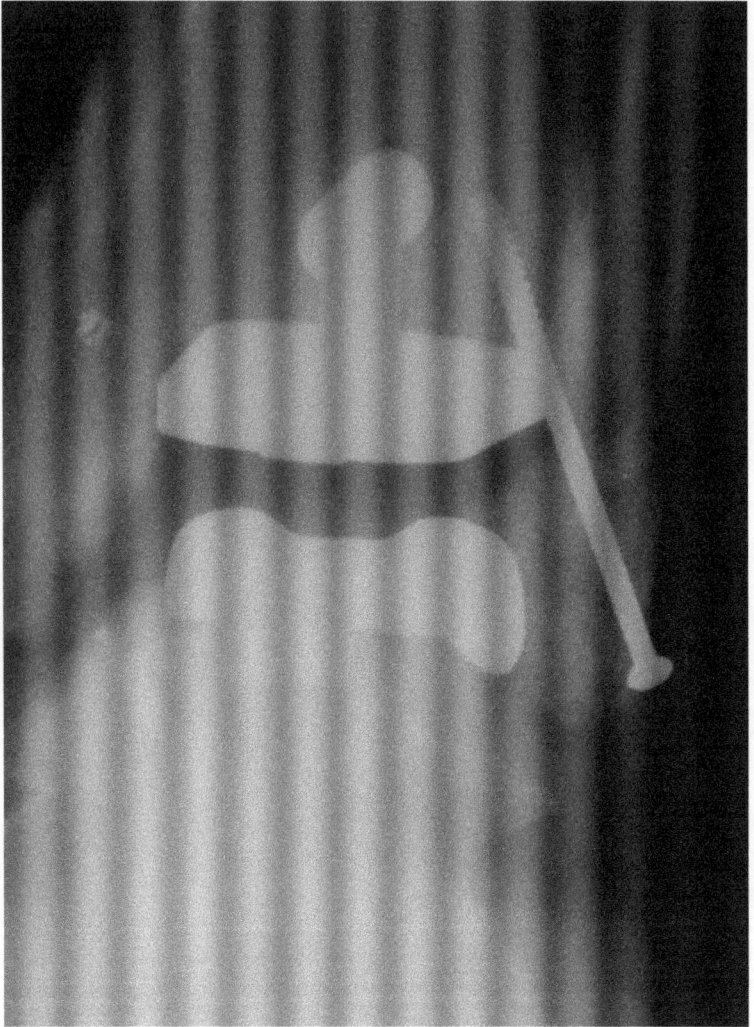

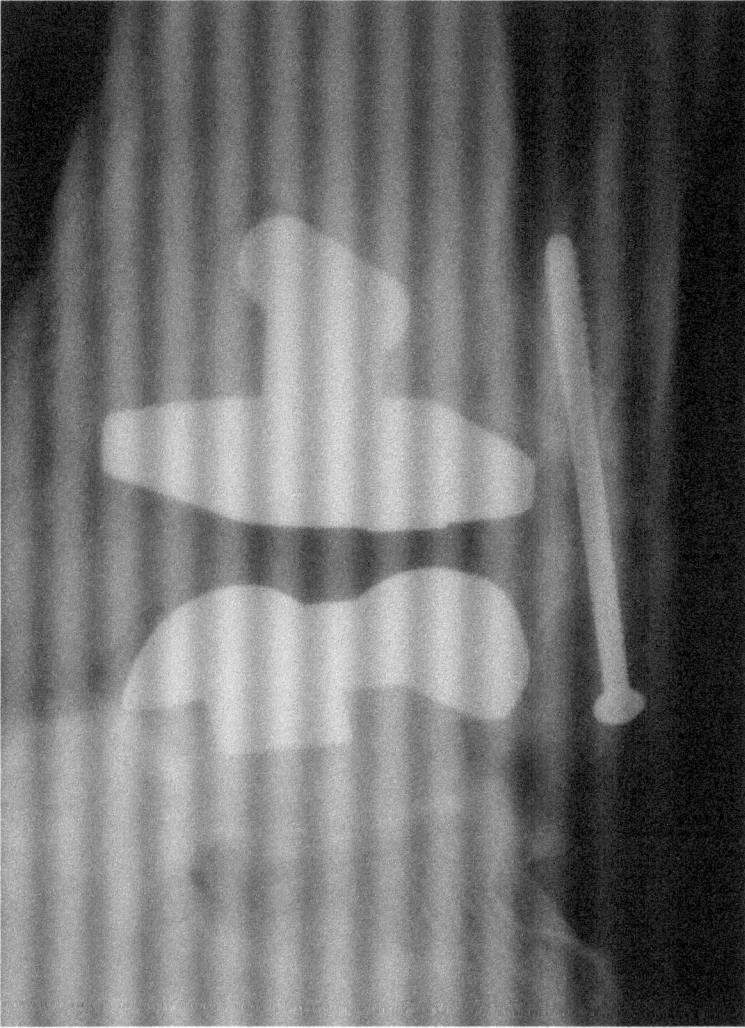

CHAPTER 13:

FORGIVENESS

The Lord had been transforming and molding me like gold is molded in many areas in my life. But there was something very crucial in my life, hidden in my heart which He will use to take me to another dimension. I lacked forgiving some things that happened at the beginning of our ministry within the church. People and families who reviled us as pastors and the leaders of the church. That part of my life and heart needed to die if I was to be an instrument in His hands. That part had not yet died, it was influencing me.

Many times we say to ourselves that we forgive, but it's not true and we deceive ourselves so we become physically and mentally ill. When God started changing my life I was unable to preach about forgiveness because I had not forgiven. How would it be possible for me to speak about forgiveness if I did not forgive? The Lord had to work in my heart in order for me to forgive my husband's family and people who attended our church that caused so much harm. I needed to put that area in His hands in order for Him to take me to other levels of understanding. Upon doing so, I crumbled before His presence and my life continued to change more. Now I can say thank you Lord because my heart is clean before you.

How great is the Lord that after five years had past of the

family conflicts, it pleased the Lord that our church worship dance group "Jabneel" be invited to my husband's family church. I felt at peace in being able to greet that family and I thank God that He had healed me so I can testify of the calling God placed in my life.

It's very important to forgive, do you know why? Because The Lord forgives you every second, minute and hour of everyday. The Lord says in His word to "forgive seventy times seven", meaning it doesn't matter what has been done to offend you, forgive, much more was done to the Lord than what has been done to you. What has kept me firm and strong in the Lord is that every time that I had gone through surgeries or processes in my life He reminds me that it was done to Him before it was done to me.

There's a verse I would like you to make your own:

> *"Above all else, guard your heart, for everything you do flows from it."*
> **Proverbs 4:23 (NIV)**

What it means is no matter what others have done to you, do not allow your heart to be blemished or be fill with resentment or bitterness. Above all things guard your heart and surrender everything to God.

CHAPTER 14:

THE OBEDIENCE

The meaning of obedience is to comply with the will of the person who orders. In this case, God is who orders and directs your life. It means acceptance of the law and will established by God.

> *"It is the Lord your God you must follow, and him you must revere. Keep his commands and obey him; serve him and hold fast to him".*
> **Deuteronomy 13:4 (NIV)**

One of the most important things for God is obedience. If you are not obedient to what He wants to do you're going to suffer the consequences. And one thing is if there is no obedience there is no sacrifice. Yet, you can make sacrifices but without obedience, it's all in vain. It is my testimony for being disobedient and for not responding to the Lord for the call he had over my life, that from one day to the next I saw myself in chaos and thinking I was going to die.

I couldn't believe what I was going through and the immense pain in my leg. But if it had not been so, I would not have been obedient to the Lord. Now let me tell you, God loves you, but when you ignore Him and you're not obedient knowing He has a purpose with you, you are going to pay the consequences. God doesn't want sacrifices from you if you are not obedient. What good is it to sacrifice yourself for Him if there is no obedience?

Many Christians today think obedience is being involved in church, preaching or standing up front and singing. That is not full obedience. Obedience is when parents tell their child to clean their room and do their homework. And that the child does it even though he complains and says he won't do it. It's the same when God says to you go and preach my word, take food to this family, I want you to take over this ministry and you do it with complaints and reproaches. It's sacrifice, but not obedience. When you simply say: "yes Lord, no problem. I will do it." This is full obedience because even though you don't know how it's done; He will teach you.

There's a process of obedience every person or Christian has to endure. Brothers and sisters I have had fifteen surgeries on my leg, specifically on my ankle in a period of fifteen years. Each one of them have been with God's purpose in my life. Many times God has had me surrender in order for Him to minister my life to cleanse and remove what He finds unpleasant. The times He has had me surrender have been marvelous and victorious years because I have endured them clenched to His hand. In the beginning I failed to understand, but to make it to the goal and to victory I had to go through the process. In my experience obedience is the Lord preparing you for events which you will encounter in your trajectory. In the midst of when such things occur you will remember those words and you praise and adore Him without complaint.

I would like to share a testimony about my obedience. In 2010 the Lord had been telling me that the time was getting short before I was going to leave my secular job and now that we are in 2016, the Lord took me out of my job in 2012. The Lord had been talking to me about having a short time left at my secular job, and that He was going to take my daughters far because He had a purpose for them.

Sometimes we believe the word we receive will happen in many years or you receive the word with doubt. We can't doubt when the Lord speaks, we must come to His presence and ask for confirmation. Because if it is from Him, that word will be realized. What I want to tell you is that in less than a month my oldest daughter left for the Army, my youngest daughter moved to live in Miami, I was removed from my job and in less than four months I had to have surgery on my ankle again. In other words, the message that I received from the Lord through different servants of God was fulfilled. I won't deny my heart was saddened because I am a very active woman.

There were many people there who I cared for and I had mixed feelings, but my time there came to an end. Now God wants me full time dedicated to His work. It cost me a lot because I loved to work and interact with people. I would like to mention I didn't appeal with an attorney, I didn't go to the county to appeal the way things were done and the way they removed me. By doing so, I understood I would have fallen in disobedience.

> *"To obey is better than sacrifice,*
> *and to heed is better than the fat of rams."*
> **Samuel 15:22b (NIV)**

If there's no obedience, there's no sacrifice. WOW! But to be obedient to God we must be willing to follow the narrow path towards perfection. Because we're not perfect but we're headed towards perfection.

CHAPTER 15:

THE DESPERATION

In the 15 years since my accident happened I have suffered a lot with the 15 surgeries. I have been through frustrations, disappointments and pain, but I have learned to mature physically and spiritually. In my case the desperation comes when you're an active person and you find yourself where you cannot bathe on your own.

I couldn't get up to do anything, I had to depend completely on my husband, friends and people who came to help. Brothers and sisters even for my personal hygiene I had to depend on my husband and unrelated people. One thing I cannot complain about is that I was never without help, the Lord always sent someone to help me. In the middle of my desperation I learned to have patience. To listen to God's voice and wait on Him. I worked twelve years in a school and I was always in and out due to my surgeries.

I went to work in a wheel chair, in crutches, with a cane, with stitches, with an open wound that you could see my tendons, and with an orthopedic boot. I have to say this, even with the pain and desperation I fulfilled my secular job responsibilities.

With the church was the same. If I went to work in those conditions how would I not go to the house of the Lord?

When you have passion for God in your heart it doesn't matter how you feel physically, you will give Him your all. I had to depend on my children to bring me something to eat. Many times the food was late and cold. Other occasions, I learned to be grateful with whatever was brought to me. Brothers and sisters many times people are too picky with the food in general and we have to learn to eat what's available. We have to be grateful. I was desperate because I had to accept my limitations and understand I couldn't do anything at home due to the condition of my ankle.

> *"Praise be to the Lord, to God our Savior,*
> *who daily bears our burdens."*
> **Psalms 68:19 (NIV)**

CHAPTER 16:

THE FRUSTRATION

From one day that I was painting the ceiling of my balcony, and I fell my life changed completely. That day was the mark; it was the key to my transformation. I was frustrated to find myself incapacitated of a leg with much pain helpless to do anything. The pain was so strong I couldn't even balance on my good foot and crutches, especially with such an active will. I felt frustrated for not being able to go to church and take part with my brothers and sisters, not being able to help my husband at home not even with the cooking part. Sometimes many of us, especially women we fuss about having to clean, cook, and work outside the home and many other things. But let me say that when you find yourself impotent, you'll find you're not able to handle any of your needs.

As time passes and your body begins to recover and simply picking up a book, a trash bag, or clean a table may be the only thing you can do that day. Give thanks to God for that, because he granted you happiness, joy and strength to do it. I was grateful to God for what little I was able to do even If I couldn't walk. I remember that when I had the rods stuck to my leg I cooked while in a wheel chair. WOW! You'd be marveled at what God allows you to do and what you can achieve. I remember not being able to walk I sat on the edge of the bed with my leg up high ironing my husband's clothes. Brothers and sisters nothing is impossible when you have the will to push forward. I don't mean to be rude, but many people find an excuse not to show up to work or church. "Oh, I have a headache, oh my back hurts, my pinky hurts!" At the end they are just excuses offered to the Lord. Later they ask themselves: "Lord, where are my blessings? Where's what you promised me?" Let me say you're not going to see them until you have made the commitment and have intimacy with the Lord.

I felt frustrated with my children having expectations of me and not being able to fulfill them. How many times I cried in pain for finding myself in this condition and not being able to do anything but pray and worship to my God. This is why when you are frustrated with your life all you can do is pray, put it in God's hand and worship Him! Brothers and sisters let me say, what transformed my life apart from the accident was my worship and praise to God. That's where He ministered and started changing my life.

> *For the Lamb at the center of the throne will be their shepherd;*
> *"He will lead them to springs of living water. And God will*
> *wipe away every tear from their eyes."*
> **Revelation 7:17 (NIV)**

CHAPTER 17:

THE LONELINESS

When I had my accident fifteen years ago I felt very lonely although I had my husband and children by my side one hundred percent. Yet there was an emptiness that I did not understand. I couldn't explain why I would cry in pain, but besides the pain I would cry for any little thing even when watching a movie. It was like if I was living what I was watching. Many people called me to see how I was doing, to provide comfort and others to get an update on my situation. In moments like these be very cautious with whom you speak and vent to, not everyone has your best interest at heart.

When I met with the Lord through this accident, I felt different even though I didn't understand things that occurred to me. I truly felt the Lord starting to fill the void in my heart, I didn't feel the gigantic solitude in my life. Many times I felt lonely because I didn't have anyone to speak to, but I was never alone, Christ was by my side every step of the way. One of the things that helped in my solitude was the Christian songs of praise and worship. WOW! I really started to know God through worship and praise, brothers and sisters that's where the Lord began ministering my life in a special way. The Lord will never leave you, usually we are the ones who leave Him. If at this very moment you find yourself in solitude, just praise God! Start to praise and seek Him and you will see how your life will change.

> *Then you will call, and the Lord will answer;*
> *you will cry for help, and he will say: Here am I.*
> **Isaiah 58:9a (NIV)**

CONCLUSION

B rothers and sisters no matter what situation you may be going through, let it be sickness, difficulties with your family, trouble at work or any other issue there's always a solution. And it's called Jesus Christ.

Author:

Pastor Ana Cecilia Dávila